50 Satisfying Healthy Eating Recipes

By: Kelly Johnson

Table of Contents

- Grilled Chicken with Quinoa Salad
- Sweet Potato and Black Bean Tacos
- Mediterranean Chickpea Salad
- Zucchini Noodles with Pesto
- Roasted Salmon with Asparagus
- Veggie-Packed Lentil Soup
- Avocado Toast with Poached Egg
- Baked Chicken Parmesan with Zoodles
- Cauliflower Fried Rice
- Turkey and Sweet Potato Meatballs
- Buddha Bowl with Hummus
- Grilled Shrimp and Veggie Skewers
- Spaghetti Squash Primavera
- Chicken and Vegetable Stir-Fry
- Roasted Chickpea and Avocado Salad
- Quinoa-Stuffed Bell Peppers
- Spicy Roasted Cauliflower
- Sweet Potato and Kale Frittata
- Veggie-Packed Quinoa Bowls
- Shrimp and Broccoli Stir-Fry
- Grilled Tofu with Avocado Salsa
- Smashed Avocado and Tomato Toast
- Eggplant Parmesan with Zucchini Noodles
- Grilled Chicken Salad with Avocado
- Baked Falafel with Tahini Sauce
- Veggie Burger with Sweet Potato Fries
- Lemon Garlic Roasted Chicken Thighs
- Cauliflower and Chickpea Buddha Bowl
- Tofu Stir-Fry with Brown Rice
- Spicy Black Bean and Quinoa Chili
- Baked Salmon with Mango Salsa
- Lentil and Spinach Curry
- Roasted Sweet Potato and Brussels Sprouts
- Grilled Veggie and Quinoa Wraps
- Avocado and Tuna Salad Lettuce Wraps

- Spaghetti Squash with Marinara Sauce
- Miso Glazed Tofu with Veggies
- Chickpea and Spinach Curry
- Grilled Veggie and Hummus Wrap
- Roasted Chicken with Sweet Potatoes
- Veggie-Packed Smoothie Bowl
- Turkey and Spinach Stuffed Peppers
- Pesto Zoodles with Cherry Tomatoes
- Broccoli and Cheddar Stuffed Chicken
- Baked Tilapia with Lemon and Herbs
- Roasted Beet and Goat Cheese Salad
- Grilled Portobello Mushrooms with Feta
- Spicy Sriracha Roasted Cauliflower
- Chicken and Avocado Lettuce Wraps
- Zucchini Fritters with Greek Yogurt

Grilled Chicken with Quinoa Salad

Ingredients:

- 2 chicken breasts
- 1 cup quinoa
- 2 cups water or chicken broth
- 1 cucumber, diced
- 1/2 red onion, diced
- 1 cup cherry tomatoes, halved
- 1/4 cup feta cheese, crumbled
- 2 tablespoons olive oil
- 1 tablespoon lemon juice
- 1 teaspoon dried oregano
- Salt and pepper to taste

Instructions:

1. Cook quinoa according to package instructions using water or chicken broth for extra flavor. Let it cool.
2. Season chicken breasts with salt, pepper, and olive oil. Grill over medium heat for 6-7 minutes on each side until fully cooked.
3. In a large bowl, combine the cooled quinoa with cucumber, onion, tomatoes, and feta.
4. Drizzle with olive oil, lemon juice, oregano, salt, and pepper, and toss to combine.
5. Slice the grilled chicken and serve on top of the quinoa salad.

Sweet Potato and Black Bean Tacos

Ingredients:

- 2 medium sweet potatoes, peeled and diced
- 1 can black beans, drained and rinsed
- 1 tablespoon olive oil
- 1 teaspoon cumin
- 1 teaspoon chili powder
- Salt and pepper to taste
- 8 small corn tortillas
- 1/2 cup avocado, sliced
- 1/4 cup cilantro, chopped
- 1/4 cup sour cream or Greek yogurt (optional)
- Lime wedges for serving

Instructions:

1. Preheat the oven to 400°F (200°C). Toss the sweet potato cubes with olive oil, cumin, chili powder, salt, and pepper.
2. Roast the sweet potatoes on a baking sheet for 25-30 minutes until tender and slightly crispy.
3. Heat the black beans in a small saucepan over medium heat.
4. Warm the tortillas in a dry skillet or microwave.
5. Assemble the tacos by placing roasted sweet potatoes and black beans on each tortilla.
6. Top with avocado, cilantro, a dollop of sour cream or yogurt, and a squeeze of lime juice. Serve immediately.

Mediterranean Chickpea Salad

Ingredients:

- 1 can chickpeas, drained and rinsed
- 1 cucumber, diced
- 1/2 red onion, finely chopped
- 1 cup cherry tomatoes, halved
- 1/4 cup Kalamata olives, pitted and chopped
- 1/4 cup feta cheese, crumbled
- 1 tablespoon olive oil
- 2 tablespoons red wine vinegar
- 1 teaspoon dried oregano
- Salt and pepper to taste

Instructions:

1. In a large bowl, combine chickpeas, cucumber, onion, tomatoes, olives, and feta.
2. In a small bowl, whisk together olive oil, red wine vinegar, oregano, salt, and pepper.
3. Pour the dressing over the salad and toss to combine.
4. Serve chilled or at room temperature as a light meal or side dish.

Zucchini Noodles with Pesto

Ingredients:

- 2 large zucchinis, spiralized into noodles
- 1 cup fresh basil leaves
- 1/4 cup pine nuts
- 2 cloves garlic
- 1/4 cup Parmesan cheese, grated
- 1/4 cup olive oil
- Salt and pepper to taste

Instructions:

1. For the pesto, combine basil, pine nuts, garlic, Parmesan, olive oil, salt, and pepper in a food processor. Pulse until smooth.
2. In a skillet, sauté zucchini noodles over medium heat for 2-3 minutes until just tender.
3. Toss the cooked zucchini noodles with the pesto until evenly coated.
4. Serve immediately, topped with additional Parmesan if desired.

Roasted Salmon with Asparagus

Ingredients:

- 2 salmon fillets
- 1 bunch asparagus, trimmed
- 1 tablespoon olive oil
- 1 tablespoon lemon juice
- 1 teaspoon garlic powder
- Salt and pepper to taste
- Lemon wedges for serving

Instructions:

1. Preheat the oven to 400°F (200°C).
2. Place the salmon fillets and asparagus on a baking sheet. Drizzle with olive oil, lemon juice, garlic powder, salt, and pepper.
3. Roast for 12-15 minutes, or until the salmon flakes easily with a fork and the asparagus is tender.
4. Serve with lemon wedges and enjoy.

Veggie-Packed Lentil Soup

Ingredients:

- 1 cup dried lentils, rinsed
- 2 carrots, diced
- 2 celery stalks, diced
- 1 onion, chopped
- 3 cloves garlic, minced
- 1 zucchini, diced
- 1 can diced tomatoes
- 4 cups vegetable broth
- 1 teaspoon cumin
- 1 teaspoon turmeric
- Salt and pepper to taste
- Fresh parsley for garnish

Instructions:

1. In a large pot, sauté onion, carrots, celery, and garlic over medium heat for 5 minutes until softened.
2. Add the zucchini, tomatoes, lentils, vegetable broth, cumin, turmeric, salt, and pepper.
3. Bring to a boil, then reduce heat and simmer for 30-40 minutes, or until the lentils are tender.
4. Garnish with fresh parsley and serve.

Avocado Toast with Poached Egg

Ingredients:

- 2 slices whole grain or sourdough bread
- 1 ripe avocado
- 2 eggs
- Salt and pepper to taste
- Red pepper flakes (optional)
- Fresh herbs (optional)

Instructions:

1. Toast the bread slices until golden brown.
2. In a small saucepan, bring water to a simmer and gently crack the eggs into the water. Poach for about 3-4 minutes for soft yolks, or longer for firmer eggs.
3. Mash the avocado in a bowl and season with salt and pepper.
4. Spread the mashed avocado on the toasted bread and top with a poached egg.
5. Sprinkle with red pepper flakes and fresh herbs, if desired. Serve immediately.

Baked Chicken Parmesan with Zoodles

Ingredients:

- 2 chicken breasts, breaded and baked
- 2 zucchini, spiralized into noodles
- 1 cup marinara sauce
- 1/2 cup mozzarella cheese, shredded
- 1/4 cup Parmesan cheese, grated
- 1 tablespoon olive oil
- Salt and pepper to taste

Instructions:

1. Preheat the oven to 375°F (190°C). Bread and bake the chicken breasts until golden and cooked through (about 20-25 minutes).
2. While the chicken is baking, heat olive oil in a skillet over medium heat. Sauté the zucchini noodles for 2-3 minutes until tender.
3. Once the chicken is cooked, spoon marinara sauce over each breast, then top with mozzarella and Parmesan.
4. Return the chicken to the oven for 5 minutes, until the cheese melts.
5. Serve the chicken over the zoodles and enjoy.

Cauliflower Fried Rice

Ingredients:

- 1 medium cauliflower, grated into rice-sized pieces
- 1 tablespoon sesame oil
- 2 eggs, scrambled
- 1/2 cup frozen peas and carrots
- 1/4 cup soy sauce (or coconut aminos)
- 2 cloves garlic, minced
- 2 green onions, chopped
- Salt and pepper to taste

Instructions:

1. In a large skillet or wok, heat sesame oil over medium-high heat. Add garlic and cook for 1 minute.
2. Add the peas and carrots and cook for 3-4 minutes until tender.
3. Push the vegetables to the side and scramble the eggs in the same skillet.
4. Add the cauliflower rice to the skillet and cook for 5-7 minutes, stirring occasionally.
5. Add soy sauce, green onions, salt, and pepper. Stir to combine and serve.

Turkey and Sweet Potato Meatballs

Ingredients:

- 1 lb ground turkey
- 1 medium sweet potato, cooked and mashed
- 1/4 cup breadcrumbs
- 1 egg
- 1 teaspoon garlic powder
- 1 teaspoon dried oregano
- Salt and pepper to taste
- Olive oil for frying

Instructions:

1. Preheat the oven to 375°F (190°C).
2. In a bowl, mix the ground turkey, mashed sweet potato, breadcrumbs, egg, garlic powder, oregano, salt, and pepper.
3. Shape the mixture into small meatballs and place them on a baking sheet.
4. Bake for 20-25 minutes, until the meatballs are cooked through and golden brown.
5. Serve with your favorite dipping sauce or as a main dish.

Buddha Bowl with Hummus

Ingredients:

- 1 cup cooked quinoa or brown rice
- 1/2 cup roasted sweet potatoes, cubed
- 1/2 cup chickpeas, roasted or canned
- 1/2 cup cucumber, sliced
- 1/4 cup shredded carrots
- 1/2 avocado, sliced
- 2 tablespoons hummus
- 1 tablespoon olive oil
- Salt and pepper to taste
- Lemon wedges for serving

Instructions:

1. In a bowl, arrange a base of quinoa or brown rice.
2. Add the roasted sweet potatoes, chickpeas, cucumber, carrots, and avocado in separate sections around the bowl.
3. Top with a spoonful of hummus in the center.
4. Drizzle with olive oil, season with salt and pepper, and serve with lemon wedges on the side.

Grilled Shrimp and Veggie Skewers

Ingredients:

- 1 lb shrimp, peeled and deveined
- 1 zucchini, sliced into rounds
- 1 red bell pepper, cut into chunks
- 1 red onion, cut into chunks
- 1 tablespoon olive oil
- 1 teaspoon garlic powder
- 1 teaspoon smoked paprika
- Salt and pepper to taste
- Lemon wedges for serving

Instructions:

1. Preheat the grill to medium-high heat.
2. Thread the shrimp, zucchini, bell pepper, and onion onto skewers.
3. In a small bowl, mix olive oil, garlic powder, smoked paprika, salt, and pepper. Brush the mixture onto the skewers.
4. Grill the skewers for 2-3 minutes on each side until the shrimp are cooked through and the vegetables are tender.
5. Serve with lemon wedges.

Spaghetti Squash Primavera

Ingredients:

- 1 medium spaghetti squash
- 1 tablespoon olive oil
- 1 cup cherry tomatoes, halved
- 1/2 red onion, thinly sliced
- 1 zucchini, sliced
- 1/2 cup bell pepper, sliced
- 2 cloves garlic, minced
- 1/4 cup fresh basil, chopped
- Salt and pepper to taste
- Parmesan cheese (optional)

Instructions:

1. Preheat the oven to 400°F (200°C).
2. Cut the spaghetti squash in half, remove the seeds, and drizzle with olive oil. Roast face down on a baking sheet for 30-40 minutes until tender.
3. While the squash is roasting, heat olive oil in a large pan and sauté the onion, zucchini, bell pepper, and garlic for 5-7 minutes until tender.
4. Add the cherry tomatoes and cook for another 2 minutes. Season with salt and pepper.
5. Once the squash is done, use a fork to scrape out the strands.
6. Toss the spaghetti squash with the sautéed vegetables and fresh basil. Top with Parmesan, if desired, and serve.

Chicken and Vegetable Stir-Fry

Ingredients:

- 1 lb chicken breast, thinly sliced
- 1 tablespoon olive oil
- 1 bell pepper, sliced
- 1 cup broccoli florets
- 1 carrot, julienned
- 1/2 onion, sliced
- 2 cloves garlic, minced
- 1/4 cup soy sauce (or coconut aminos)
- 1 tablespoon honey
- 1 teaspoon sesame oil
- 1 teaspoon ginger, grated

Instructions:

1. Heat olive oil in a large skillet or wok over medium-high heat. Add the chicken and cook for 5-7 minutes until browned and cooked through. Remove from the skillet.
2. In the same skillet, add a bit more olive oil and sauté the bell pepper, broccoli, carrot, and onion for 3-4 minutes until slightly tender.
3. Add the garlic, soy sauce, honey, sesame oil, and ginger. Stir to combine.
4. Return the chicken to the skillet and toss everything together for another 2-3 minutes.
5. Serve hot over rice or quinoa.

Roasted Chickpea and Avocado Salad

Ingredients:

- 1 can chickpeas, drained and rinsed
- 1 tablespoon olive oil
- 1 teaspoon cumin
- 1 teaspoon paprika
- Salt and pepper to taste
- 1 avocado, diced
- 1/2 cucumber, diced
- 1/4 cup red onion, thinly sliced
- 1 tablespoon lemon juice
- Fresh parsley for garnish

Instructions:

1. Preheat the oven to 400°F (200°C).
2. Toss chickpeas with olive oil, cumin, paprika, salt, and pepper. Spread on a baking sheet and roast for 25-30 minutes until crispy.
3. In a bowl, combine avocado, cucumber, red onion, and lemon juice.
4. Once the chickpeas are roasted, add them to the salad and toss gently.
5. Garnish with fresh parsley and serve.

Quinoa-Stuffed Bell Peppers

Ingredients:

- 4 bell peppers, tops cut off and seeds removed
- 1 cup quinoa, cooked
- 1 can black beans, drained and rinsed
- 1/2 cup corn kernels (fresh or frozen)
- 1 teaspoon cumin
- 1 teaspoon chili powder
- Salt and pepper to taste
- 1/2 cup shredded cheese (optional)

Instructions:

1. Preheat the oven to 375°F (190°C).
2. In a bowl, combine cooked quinoa, black beans, corn, cumin, chili powder, salt, and pepper.
3. Stuff the bell peppers with the quinoa mixture and place them in a baking dish.
4. If using, sprinkle cheese on top of each stuffed pepper.
5. Cover with foil and bake for 30 minutes, then remove the foil and bake for an additional 10-15 minutes until the peppers are tender.

Spicy Roasted Cauliflower

Ingredients:

- 1 head of cauliflower, cut into florets
- 2 tablespoons olive oil
- 1 teaspoon smoked paprika
- 1/2 teaspoon cayenne pepper
- 1 teaspoon garlic powder
- Salt and pepper to taste
- Fresh parsley for garnish

Instructions:

1. Preheat the oven to 425°F (220°C).
2. Toss cauliflower florets with olive oil, smoked paprika, cayenne, garlic powder, salt, and pepper.
3. Spread the cauliflower in a single layer on a baking sheet and roast for 20-25 minutes, until golden and tender.
4. Garnish with fresh parsley and serve.

Sweet Potato and Kale Frittata

Ingredients:

- 1 large sweet potato, peeled and diced
- 1 tablespoon olive oil
- 2 cups kale, chopped
- 6 large eggs
- 1/4 cup milk (or dairy-free alternative)
- Salt and pepper to taste
- 1/4 cup feta cheese (optional)

Instructions:

1. Preheat the oven to 375°F (190°C).
2. In a skillet, heat olive oil over medium heat and sauté the sweet potato for 7-10 minutes until tender.
3. Add the kale and cook for another 3-4 minutes until wilted.
4. In a bowl, whisk together eggs, milk, salt, and pepper.
5. Pour the egg mixture into the skillet over the vegetables. Cook on the stove for 3-4 minutes until the edges begin to set.
6. Transfer the skillet to the oven and bake for 10-15 minutes, until the center is set.
7. Top with feta cheese if desired and serve warm.

Veggie-Packed Quinoa Bowls

Ingredients:

- 1 cup cooked quinoa
- 1/2 cup roasted sweet potatoes, cubed
- 1/2 cup roasted broccoli florets
- 1/4 cup red cabbage, shredded
- 1/4 cup avocado, sliced
- 2 tablespoons tahini dressing
- Lemon wedges for serving

Instructions:

1. In a bowl, layer cooked quinoa, sweet potatoes, broccoli, red cabbage, and avocado.
2. Drizzle with tahini dressing and squeeze lemon juice over the top.
3. Serve immediately for a nutritious, filling meal.

Shrimp and Broccoli Stir-Fry

Ingredients:

- 1 lb shrimp, peeled and deveined
- 1 tablespoon olive oil
- 2 cups broccoli florets
- 1 red bell pepper, sliced
- 2 cloves garlic, minced
- 1 tablespoon soy sauce (or coconut aminos)
- 1 tablespoon honey
- 1 teaspoon sesame oil
- 1/2 teaspoon ginger, grated
- Cooked rice for serving

Instructions:

1. In a large skillet or wok, heat olive oil over medium-high heat. Add the shrimp and cook for 2-3 minutes until pink and cooked through. Remove and set aside.
2. In the same skillet, sauté broccoli and bell pepper for 3-4 minutes until tender.
3. Add garlic, soy sauce, honey, sesame oil, and ginger, and stir to combine.
4. Return the shrimp to the skillet and toss everything together for another 2 minutes.
5. Serve the stir-fry over cooked rice and enjoy.

Grilled Tofu with Avocado Salsa

Ingredients:

- 1 block firm tofu, pressed and sliced
- 1 tablespoon olive oil
- 1 teaspoon soy sauce
- 1 teaspoon garlic powder
- 1 teaspoon smoked paprika
- Salt and pepper to taste
- 1 avocado, diced
- 1/2 red onion, finely diced
- 1/2 cup cherry tomatoes, halved
- 1 tablespoon cilantro, chopped
- Juice of 1 lime

Instructions:

1. Preheat the grill or grill pan over medium heat.
2. In a small bowl, mix olive oil, soy sauce, garlic powder, paprika, salt, and pepper. Brush the tofu slices with the marinade.
3. Grill the tofu for 4-5 minutes on each side until golden and crispy.
4. In a separate bowl, mix avocado, onion, tomatoes, cilantro, and lime juice. Season with salt and pepper.
5. Serve the grilled tofu with a generous scoop of avocado salsa on top.

Smashed Avocado and Tomato Toast

Ingredients:

- 2 slices whole grain bread, toasted
- 1 avocado, mashed
- 1/2 cup cherry tomatoes, halved
- 1 tablespoon lemon juice
- Salt and pepper to taste
- Red pepper flakes (optional)

Instructions:

1. Toast the bread slices to your liking.
2. Mash the avocado with lemon juice, salt, and pepper.
3. Spread the mashed avocado evenly on the toasted bread.
4. Top with halved cherry tomatoes and a sprinkle of red pepper flakes if desired.
5. Serve immediately as a delicious breakfast or snack.

Eggplant Parmesan with Zucchini Noodles

Ingredients:

- 2 medium eggplants, sliced into 1/2-inch rounds
- 1 cup marinara sauce
- 1/2 cup mozzarella cheese, shredded
- 1/4 cup Parmesan cheese, grated
- 2 medium zucchinis, spiralized
- 1/2 cup breadcrumbs (use gluten-free if needed)
- 1 egg, beaten
- Olive oil for frying

Instructions:

1. Preheat the oven to 375°F (190°C).
2. Dip each eggplant slice into the beaten egg, then coat with breadcrumbs. Heat olive oil in a skillet over medium heat and fry the eggplant slices until golden, about 2-3 minutes per side. Transfer to a paper towel to drain.
3. In a baking dish, layer the fried eggplant slices with marinara sauce and cheese. Repeat layers until all the eggplant is used.
4. Bake for 20-25 minutes until bubbly and golden.
5. While the eggplant is baking, sauté the zucchini noodles in a pan with a little olive oil for 2-3 minutes until tender.
6. Serve the eggplant Parmesan on top of the zucchini noodles.

Grilled Chicken Salad with Avocado

Ingredients:

- 2 chicken breasts, grilled and sliced
- 1 avocado, sliced
- 2 cups mixed greens (spinach, arugula, etc.)
- 1/2 cucumber, sliced
- 1/4 red onion, thinly sliced
- 1/4 cup feta cheese (optional)
- 2 tablespoons olive oil
- 1 tablespoon balsamic vinegar
- Salt and pepper to taste

Instructions:

1. Grill the chicken breasts over medium heat for 6-7 minutes on each side until cooked through. Slice into thin strips.
2. In a large bowl, combine the mixed greens, cucumber, red onion, and avocado.
3. Drizzle with olive oil and balsamic vinegar, then season with salt and pepper.
4. Top the salad with grilled chicken slices and feta cheese if desired.
5. Serve immediately for a refreshing and healthy meal.

Baked Falafel with Tahini Sauce

Ingredients for Falafel:

- 1 can chickpeas, drained and rinsed
- 1/4 cup onion, chopped
- 2 cloves garlic, minced
- 1/4 cup fresh parsley, chopped
- 1 teaspoon cumin
- 1 teaspoon coriander
- Salt and pepper to taste
- 2 tablespoons flour (or chickpea flour for gluten-free)
- Olive oil for baking

Ingredients for Tahini Sauce:

- 1/4 cup tahini
- 2 tablespoons lemon juice
- 1 tablespoon olive oil
- 1 clove garlic, minced
- Water to thin the sauce
- Salt to taste

Instructions:

1. Preheat the oven to 400°F (200°C). Line a baking sheet with parchment paper.
2. In a food processor, combine the chickpeas, onion, garlic, parsley, cumin, coriander, salt, and pepper. Pulse until combined but still slightly chunky. Add flour and mix.
3. Form the mixture into small balls and place them on the prepared baking sheet. Drizzle with olive oil.
4. Bake for 25-30 minutes, flipping halfway through, until golden and crispy.
5. For the tahini sauce, whisk together tahini, lemon juice, olive oil, garlic, and salt. Add water a little at a time until the desired consistency is reached.
6. Serve the falafel with tahini sauce on the side.

Veggie Burger with Sweet Potato Fries

Ingredients for Veggie Burger:

- 1 can black beans, drained and rinsed
- 1/2 cup breadcrumbs
- 1/4 cup grated carrot
- 1/4 cup corn kernels
- 1 teaspoon cumin
- Salt and pepper to taste
- 1 egg (or flax egg for vegan)
- Olive oil for cooking

Ingredients for Sweet Potato Fries:

- 2 large sweet potatoes, peeled and cut into fries
- 1 tablespoon olive oil
- 1 teaspoon paprika
- Salt and pepper to taste

Instructions:

1. Preheat the oven to 425°F (220°C). Toss sweet potato fries with olive oil, paprika, salt, and pepper. Spread them on a baking sheet and bake for 25-30 minutes, flipping halfway through, until crispy.
2. For the veggie burgers, mash the black beans in a bowl and add breadcrumbs, carrot, corn, cumin, salt, pepper, and egg. Mix until well combined.
3. Form the mixture into patties and cook in a skillet over medium heat with a bit of olive oil for 4-5 minutes per side until golden and crispy.
4. Serve the veggie burgers with your choice of toppings (lettuce, tomato, etc.) and sweet potato fries on the side.

Lemon Garlic Roasted Chicken Thighs

Ingredients:

- 4 chicken thighs, bone-in and skin-on
- 2 tablespoons olive oil
- 4 cloves garlic, minced
- Juice of 1 lemon
- 1 teaspoon dried thyme
- Salt and pepper to taste

Instructions:

1. Preheat the oven to 400°F (200°C).
2. In a small bowl, mix olive oil, garlic, lemon juice, thyme, salt, and pepper.
3. Rub the chicken thighs with the mixture and place them on a baking sheet.
4. Roast for 35-40 minutes, until the chicken is crispy on the outside and cooked through.
5. Serve with a side of roasted vegetables or a salad.

Cauliflower and Chickpea Buddha Bowl

Ingredients:

- 1 head cauliflower, cut into florets
- 1 can chickpeas, drained and rinsed
- 1 tablespoon olive oil
- 1 teaspoon turmeric
- 1 teaspoon cumin
- Salt and pepper to taste
- 1 cup cooked quinoa or rice
- 1 avocado, sliced
- 1 tablespoon tahini

Instructions:

1. Preheat the oven to 425°F (220°C).
2. Toss the cauliflower florets and chickpeas with olive oil, turmeric, cumin, salt, and pepper. Spread them on a baking sheet and roast for 25-30 minutes.
3. In a bowl, layer the quinoa or rice, roasted cauliflower and chickpeas, and sliced avocado.
4. Drizzle with tahini and serve.

Tofu Stir-Fry with Brown Rice

Ingredients:

- 1 block firm tofu, pressed and cubed
- 1 tablespoon soy sauce (or coconut aminos)
- 1 tablespoon sesame oil
- 1 bell pepper, sliced
- 1/2 cup broccoli florets
- 1/2 onion, sliced
- 2 cloves garlic, minced
- 1 cup cooked brown rice
- 1 teaspoon sesame seeds

Instructions:

1. Heat sesame oil in a pan over medium heat. Add the tofu cubes and cook for 5-7 minutes until golden and crispy.
2. Add the bell pepper, broccoli, onion, and garlic. Stir-fry for another 4-5 minutes until the vegetables are tender.
3. Add the soy sauce and stir to combine.
4. Serve the stir-fry over brown rice, garnished with sesame seeds.

Spicy Black Bean and Quinoa Chili

Ingredients:

- 1 cup quinoa, rinsed
- 2 cans black beans, drained and rinsed
- 1 can diced tomatoes
- 1 onion, chopped
- 2 cloves garlic, minced
- 1 red bell pepper, chopped
- 1 jalapeño, minced (optional for spice)
- 1 tablespoon chili powder
- 1 teaspoon cumin
- 1/2 teaspoon paprika
- 2 cups vegetable broth
- 1 tablespoon olive oil
- Salt and pepper to taste

Instructions:

1. In a large pot, heat olive oil over medium heat. Add onion, garlic, bell pepper, and jalapeño. Sauté for 5 minutes until softened.
2. Stir in chili powder, cumin, paprika, salt, and pepper. Add the quinoa, black beans, diced tomatoes, and vegetable broth.
3. Bring to a boil, then reduce the heat and simmer for 20-25 minutes, stirring occasionally, until the quinoa is cooked and the chili thickens.
4. Adjust seasoning as needed and serve hot.

Baked Salmon with Mango Salsa

Ingredients for Salmon:

- 4 salmon fillets
- 1 tablespoon olive oil
- 1 lemon, sliced
- Salt and pepper to taste

Ingredients for Mango Salsa:

- 1 ripe mango, diced
- 1/2 red onion, finely chopped
- 1/2 red bell pepper, diced
- 1 tablespoon cilantro, chopped
- Juice of 1 lime
- Salt to taste

Instructions:

1. Preheat the oven to 375°F (190°C).
2. Place salmon fillets on a baking sheet lined with parchment paper. Drizzle with olive oil and season with salt and pepper. Arrange lemon slices on top of the salmon.
3. Bake for 12-15 minutes, until salmon is cooked through.
4. In a bowl, combine mango, onion, bell pepper, cilantro, lime juice, and salt to make the salsa.
5. Serve the baked salmon topped with fresh mango salsa.

Lentil and Spinach Curry

Ingredients:

- 1 cup dried lentils, rinsed
- 1 onion, chopped
- 2 cloves garlic, minced
- 1 tablespoon ginger, grated
- 1 can diced tomatoes
- 2 cups vegetable broth
- 2 cups fresh spinach
- 1 tablespoon curry powder
- 1 teaspoon turmeric
- 1 teaspoon cumin
- 1/2 teaspoon cinnamon
- 1 tablespoon olive oil
- Salt and pepper to taste

Instructions:

1. In a large pot, heat olive oil over medium heat. Add onion, garlic, and ginger. Sauté for 5 minutes until softened.
2. Stir in curry powder, turmeric, cumin, cinnamon, salt, and pepper. Cook for another minute until fragrant.
3. Add the lentils, tomatoes, and vegetable broth. Bring to a boil, then reduce to a simmer. Cook for 30-35 minutes until the lentils are tender.
4. Stir in spinach and cook until wilted, about 2 minutes.
5. Serve hot with rice or naan.

Roasted Sweet Potato and Brussels Sprouts

Ingredients:

- 2 large sweet potatoes, peeled and cubed
- 1 lb Brussels sprouts, trimmed and halved
- 2 tablespoons olive oil
- 1 teaspoon paprika
- 1/2 teaspoon garlic powder
- Salt and pepper to taste

Instructions:

1. Preheat the oven to 400°F (200°C).
2. In a large bowl, toss sweet potatoes and Brussels sprouts with olive oil, paprika, garlic powder, salt, and pepper.
3. Spread the vegetables evenly on a baking sheet. Roast for 25-30 minutes, flipping halfway through, until golden and tender.
4. Serve warm as a side dish.

Grilled Veggie and Quinoa Wraps

Ingredients:

- 1 cup cooked quinoa
- 1 zucchini, sliced
- 1 red bell pepper, sliced
- 1/2 red onion, sliced
- 1 tablespoon olive oil
- 4 large whole wheat wraps
- 2 tablespoons hummus or tahini (optional)
- Salt and pepper to taste

Instructions:

1. Preheat the grill or grill pan over medium heat.
2. Toss zucchini, bell pepper, and onion with olive oil, salt, and pepper. Grill for 4-5 minutes on each side until tender and lightly charred.
3. Lay the grilled veggies over the quinoa on the wraps. Drizzle with hummus or tahini if desired.
4. Roll up the wraps and serve.

Avocado and Tuna Salad Lettuce Wraps

Ingredients:

- 1 can tuna, drained
- 1 avocado, diced
- 1/4 red onion, finely chopped
- 1 tablespoon lemon juice
- 2 tablespoons mayonnaise or Greek yogurt
- Salt and pepper to taste
- 8 large lettuce leaves (such as butter or romaine)

Instructions:

1. In a bowl, combine tuna, avocado, red onion, lemon juice, and mayonnaise (or yogurt). Season with salt and pepper.
2. Spoon the mixture into individual lettuce leaves and serve as wraps.

Spaghetti Squash with Marinara Sauce

Ingredients:

- 1 medium spaghetti squash
- 2 cups marinara sauce
- 1 tablespoon olive oil
- Fresh basil leaves for garnish
- Salt and pepper to taste

Instructions:

1. Preheat the oven to 400°F (200°C).
2. Cut the spaghetti squash in half and remove the seeds. Drizzle with olive oil and season with salt and pepper.
3. Place the squash halves cut side down on a baking sheet. Roast for 30-35 minutes, or until tender.
4. Once roasted, use a fork to scrape out the strands of squash into a bowl.
5. Heat the marinara sauce in a pan and pour over the spaghetti squash. Garnish with fresh basil and serve.

Miso Glazed Tofu with Veggies

Ingredients:

- 1 block firm tofu, pressed and cubed
- 2 tablespoons miso paste
- 1 tablespoon soy sauce
- 1 tablespoon rice vinegar
- 1 teaspoon sesame oil
- 1 tablespoon honey or maple syrup
- 1 tablespoon sesame seeds
- 1 cup broccoli florets
- 1 red bell pepper, sliced
- 1 tablespoon olive oil

Instructions:

1. Preheat the oven to 375°F (190°C). Line a baking sheet with parchment paper.
2. In a bowl, whisk together miso paste, soy sauce, rice vinegar, sesame oil, and honey.
3. Toss the tofu cubes in the miso mixture and spread them on the baking sheet. Roast for 25-30 minutes until crispy.
4. In a skillet, heat olive oil over medium heat. Sauté broccoli and bell pepper for 5-7 minutes until tender.
5. Serve the roasted tofu over the sautéed veggies and sprinkle with sesame seeds.

Chickpea and Spinach Curry

Ingredients:

- 1 can chickpeas, drained and rinsed
- 2 cups fresh spinach
- 1 onion, chopped
- 2 cloves garlic, minced
- 1 tablespoon ginger, grated
- 1 tablespoon curry powder
- 1 teaspoon cumin
- 1 can diced tomatoes
- 1 cup coconut milk
- 1 tablespoon olive oil
- Salt and pepper to taste

Instructions:

1. In a large pot, heat olive oil over medium heat. Add onion, garlic, and ginger. Sauté for 5 minutes until softened.
2. Stir in curry powder and cumin. Cook for 1 minute.
3. Add chickpeas, tomatoes, and coconut milk. Bring to a boil, then simmer for 15-20 minutes.
4. Stir in spinach and cook until wilted.
5. Serve with rice or naan.

Grilled Veggie and Hummus Wrap

Ingredients:

- 1 zucchini, sliced
- 1 red bell pepper, sliced
- 1/2 red onion, sliced
- 1 tablespoon olive oil
- 4 large whole wheat wraps
- 1/2 cup hummus
- Salt and pepper to taste

Instructions:

1. Preheat the grill or grill pan over medium heat.
2. Toss the zucchini, bell pepper, and onion with olive oil, salt, and pepper.
3. Grill the vegetables for 4-5 minutes on each side until tender and lightly charred.
4. Spread hummus on each wrap.
5. Arrange the grilled veggies on top, roll up, and serve.

Roasted Chicken with Sweet Potatoes

Ingredients:

- 4 bone-in chicken thighs
- 2 medium sweet potatoes, peeled and cubed
- 2 tablespoons olive oil
- 1 teaspoon paprika
- 1/2 teaspoon garlic powder
- Salt and pepper to taste
- Fresh thyme or rosemary (optional)

Instructions:

1. Preheat the oven to 400°F (200°C).
2. Place the chicken thighs and sweet potatoes on a baking sheet.
3. Drizzle with olive oil and sprinkle with paprika, garlic powder, salt, and pepper.
4. Toss the sweet potatoes and coat the chicken evenly with seasonings.
5. Roast for 30-35 minutes, or until the chicken is cooked through and the sweet potatoes are tender.
6. Garnish with fresh thyme or rosemary before serving.

Veggie-Packed Smoothie Bowl

Ingredients:

- 1/2 cup spinach or kale
- 1/2 frozen banana
- 1/2 cup frozen mixed berries
- 1/4 cup almond milk (or your choice)
- 1 tablespoon peanut butter or almond butter
- Toppings: granola, sliced almonds, chia seeds, fresh fruit

Instructions:

1. Blend the spinach, banana, berries, almond milk, and peanut butter until smooth.
2. Pour the smoothie mixture into a bowl.
3. Top with granola, sliced almonds, chia seeds, and fresh fruit.
4. Serve immediately as a refreshing, nutrient-packed breakfast or snack.

Turkey and Spinach Stuffed Peppers

Ingredients:

- 4 bell peppers, tops cut off and seeds removed
- 1 lb ground turkey
- 1 onion, chopped
- 2 cloves garlic, minced
- 2 cups fresh spinach, chopped
- 1/2 cup cooked quinoa or rice
- 1 teaspoon Italian seasoning
- Salt and pepper to taste
- 1/2 cup shredded cheese (optional)

Instructions:

1. Preheat the oven to 375°F (190°C).
2. In a skillet, cook the ground turkey over medium heat until browned, breaking it apart with a spoon.
3. Add onion and garlic, and cook until softened.
4. Stir in spinach, cooked quinoa or rice, Italian seasoning, salt, and pepper. Cook for another 2 minutes until spinach wilts.
5. Stuff the peppers with the turkey mixture and place them in a baking dish.
6. Top with cheese, if desired, and bake for 25-30 minutes, until the peppers are tender.

Pesto Zoodles with Cherry Tomatoes

Ingredients:

- 2 medium zucchinis, spiralized into noodles (zoodles)
- 1 cup cherry tomatoes, halved
- 2 tablespoons pesto sauce
- 1 tablespoon olive oil
- Salt and pepper to taste
- Parmesan cheese for garnish (optional)

Instructions:

1. In a skillet, heat olive oil over medium heat. Add the zoodles and sauté for 2-3 minutes, just until tender.
2. Stir in the pesto sauce and cherry tomatoes. Cook for an additional 1-2 minutes until the tomatoes are softened.
3. Season with salt and pepper.
4. Serve warm, topped with Parmesan cheese if desired.

Broccoli and Cheddar Stuffed Chicken

Ingredients:

- 4 boneless, skinless chicken breasts
- 1 cup steamed broccoli, chopped
- 1/2 cup shredded cheddar cheese
- 1/4 cup cream cheese, softened
- 1 tablespoon olive oil
- Salt and pepper to taste

Instructions:

1. Preheat the oven to 375°F (190°C).
2. Slice a pocket into each chicken breast, being careful not to cut all the way through.
3. In a bowl, mix the steamed broccoli, cheddar cheese, and cream cheese.
4. Stuff the chicken breasts with the broccoli mixture and secure with toothpicks.
5. Heat olive oil in a skillet over medium heat. Sear the chicken breasts on both sides until golden, about 2-3 minutes per side.
6. Transfer the chicken to the oven and bake for 20-25 minutes, or until the chicken is cooked through and the filling is hot.

Baked Tilapia with Lemon and Herbs

Ingredients:

- 4 tilapia fillets
- 1 lemon, thinly sliced
- 2 tablespoons olive oil
- 1 teaspoon dried thyme
- 1 teaspoon garlic powder
- Salt and pepper to taste
- Fresh parsley for garnish

Instructions:

1. Preheat the oven to 400°F (200°C).
2. Place the tilapia fillets on a baking sheet lined with parchment paper.
3. Drizzle the fillets with olive oil and season with garlic powder, thyme, salt, and pepper.
4. Top with lemon slices and bake for 12-15 minutes, or until the fish flakes easily with a fork.
5. Garnish with fresh parsley and serve with your choice of sides.

Roasted Beet and Goat Cheese Salad

Ingredients:

- 4 medium beets, peeled and cut into wedges
- 1 tablespoon olive oil
- Salt and pepper to taste
- 4 cups mixed salad greens (arugula, spinach, etc.)
- 1/4 cup crumbled goat cheese
- 1/4 cup walnuts, toasted (optional)
- 2 tablespoons balsamic vinegar
- 1 tablespoon olive oil

Instructions:

1. Preheat the oven to 400°F (200°C).
2. Toss the beet wedges with olive oil, salt, and pepper, then place them on a baking sheet.
3. Roast the beets for 30-40 minutes, flipping halfway through, until they are tender.
4. In a large bowl, toss the salad greens with balsamic vinegar and olive oil.
5. Arrange the roasted beets on top of the greens, then sprinkle with goat cheese and toasted walnuts.
6. Serve immediately as a refreshing, earthy salad.

Grilled Portobello Mushrooms with Feta

Ingredients:

- 4 large Portobello mushroom caps, cleaned and stems removed
- 2 tablespoons olive oil
- 1 teaspoon garlic powder
- 1 teaspoon dried oregano
- Salt and pepper to taste
- 1/2 cup crumbled feta cheese
- 1 tablespoon fresh parsley, chopped (optional)

Instructions:

1. Preheat the grill or grill pan over medium heat.
2. Brush both sides of the mushroom caps with olive oil, and season with garlic powder, oregano, salt, and pepper.
3. Grill the mushrooms for 5-7 minutes per side, until tender and grill marks appear.
4. Remove from the grill and sprinkle with crumbled feta cheese.
5. Garnish with fresh parsley before serving.

Spicy Sriracha Roasted Cauliflower

Ingredients:

- 1 medium cauliflower, cut into florets
- 2 tablespoons olive oil
- 2 tablespoons Sriracha sauce
- 1 tablespoon soy sauce
- 1 teaspoon garlic powder
- Salt and pepper to taste
- Fresh cilantro for garnish (optional)

Instructions:

1. Preheat the oven to 425°F (220°C).
2. In a large bowl, toss the cauliflower florets with olive oil, Sriracha, soy sauce, garlic powder, salt, and pepper.
3. Spread the cauliflower evenly on a baking sheet.
4. Roast for 25-30 minutes, flipping halfway through, until the cauliflower is crispy on the edges and tender inside.
5. Garnish with fresh cilantro before serving for a spicy, flavorful side dish.

Chicken and Avocado Lettuce Wraps

Ingredients:

- 2 chicken breasts, cooked and shredded
- 1 ripe avocado, diced
- 1/4 cup Greek yogurt or sour cream
- 1 tablespoon lime juice
- 1 teaspoon chili powder
- Salt and pepper to taste
- 12 large lettuce leaves (e.g., Romaine or Butterhead)
- Fresh cilantro for garnish (optional)

Instructions:

1. In a bowl, mix the shredded chicken, avocado, Greek yogurt, lime juice, chili powder, salt, and pepper.
2. Gently stir to combine, making sure the avocado is evenly distributed.
3. Spoon the mixture onto the center of each lettuce leaf.
4. Garnish with fresh cilantro if desired, and serve as a light, healthy lunch or snack.

Zucchini Fritters with Greek Yogurt

Ingredients:

- 2 medium zucchinis, grated
- 1/2 cup flour (or chickpea flour for gluten-free)
- 1 egg, beaten
- 1/4 cup grated Parmesan cheese
- 2 tablespoons fresh dill, chopped (optional)
- 1 clove garlic, minced
- Salt and pepper to taste
- 2 tablespoons olive oil
- 1/2 cup Greek yogurt, for serving

Instructions:

1. Grate the zucchini and place it in a clean kitchen towel or cheesecloth. Squeeze out excess moisture.
2. In a bowl, combine the grated zucchini, flour, egg, Parmesan cheese, dill, garlic, salt, and pepper.
3. Heat olive oil in a large skillet over medium heat.
4. Drop spoonfuls of the zucchini mixture into the skillet, flattening them slightly to form fritters.
5. Cook for 2-3 minutes per side, until golden brown and crispy.
6. Serve the fritters warm, topped with a dollop of Greek yogurt for a creamy finish.

www.ingramcontent.com/pod-product-compliance
Lightning Source LLC
LaVergne TN
LVHW081502060526
838201LV00056BA/2894